Original title:
Murmurs in the Mossy Grove

Copyright © 2025 Creative Arts Management OÜ
All rights reserved.

Author: Nora Sinclair
ISBN HARDBACK: 978-1-80567-437-5
ISBN PAPERBACK: 978-1-80567-736-9

Enigma Hidden Beneath the Canopy

In the woods where secrets play,
A squirrel dressed in shades of gray,
He dances on the branches high,
While all the rabbits wonder why.

A hedgehog sings a dandy tune,
While frogs croak ballads to the moon,
They trade their jokes with careful art,
In jest, they've built a leafy mart.

The owls hold court in comical frowns,
Telling tales of lost and found,
A fox with flair, a hat askew,
Claims he's the ruler of the crew.

Beneath the canopy's embrace,
Life unfurls its whimsical grace,
With laughter echoing through the trees,
The grove's a stage, oh what a tease!

Lullabies of the Old Oak

In the arms of branches wide,
Squirrels chatter, trying to hide.
A songbird drops her shiny snack,
"Sorry!" she chirps, then takes it back.

The wind begins to play a tune,
With rustles that make leaves swoon.
A raccoon tap dances with flair,
While beetles join the music air.

Sighs of the Twilight Thicket

Crickets whisper, trying to tease,
As fireflies flicker with gentle ease.
A badger naps with dreams so bright,
Waking up to a startled fright.

A rabbit skips through dew-kissed grass,
Bumping into a snail with sass.
"Excuse me, sir, could you take heed?
My breakfast won't wait, it's quite a creed!"

The Quiet Chorus of Green

Frogs croak loud, what a commotion,
As turtles glide, causing quite the notion.
A snail zips by in a speedy race,
"Hey, slow down! You're losing grace!"

The hedgehogs giggle, hiding away,
As owls hoot jokes at the end of day.
With laughter echoing through the leaves,
Nature's humor weaves and weaves.

Shadows Dancing in the Dappled Light

Mice play hide-and-seek with sun,
While shadows chase, it's all in fun.
A chubby raccoon slips on a log,
"Next time I'll wear a better frog!"

The breeze sneezes, sends leaves in flight,
Swaying branches join the delight.
A worm wears glasses, reading a page,
"Next week's dance, I'll be center stage!"

Flutters Through the Whispering Grasses

Bunny hops and toads will squawk,
While crickets dance and jest in shock.
A fox in socks begins to prance,
Who knew the herbs could lead a dance?

The daisies laugh, the ferns all cheer,
As butterflies giggle, spreading cheer.
The daisies tell the tale of the day,
While squirrels laugh in their cheeky play.

Ramblings of the Rustic Path

A hedgehog snorts, an antelope sighs,
Why'd the chicken cross? Just to surprise!
A tortoise bets the snail a coin,
And the path hums with a leaf's coy join.

Chasing shadows, we find a frog,
Who croaks out puns beneath a log.
With every step, a chuckle grows,
Nature's silly, as everyone knows.

Portals of the Twilit Shrubbery

A wizard's hat on a stone so round,
Who knows what magic lies to be found?
Owl in specs, reading a book,
Critiquing stars with just a look.

While gnomes giggle, knead the clay,
Crafting jokes in a whimsical way.
Beneath the moon, tales of delight,
Where evenings whisper in soft moonlight.

Harmony in the Woodland Quiet

A raccoon sings with a rusty tune,
Beneath the gaze of a playful moon.
With trees that sway in a secret dance,
They beckon us to join the chance.

Chipmunks chatter, sharing a jest,
In the calm, they all feel blessed.
The breeze joins in, a playful tease,
In quiet harmony, we laugh with ease.

Whispers Beneath the Canopy

In the trees, the squirrels chatter,
As they plot and scheme for shiny matter.
A raccoon with a mask, so sly and clever,
Stealing snacks, he says, "I'll stop never!"

Under branches, a rabbit sneezes,
While a bear munches on caramel cheese.
The echo of laughter from the playful winds,
As shadows dance where the fun begins.

Secrets of the Ancient Woodland

Whispers float from the wise old trees,
"You call that a dance? It's more like a breeze!"
With giggles, the fawns leap in delight,
While gnomes juggle acorns under moonlight.

A turtle in spectacles gives a slow cheer,
"I'll race you to lunch, but I won't disappear!"
The fox, with a grin, takes the bait for a game,
"You can run, but I'll always be the same!"

Echoes in the Emerald Shade

A frog croaks out a ribbit grand,
While chatting with a turtle who can't understand.
"Hop this way!" shouts the grasshopper spry,
"Or stay where it's safe, not giving a try!"

The mushrooms giggle in their little nook,
As an owl pretends to read a book.
Chattering leaves join the banter with glee,
Spinning tales of who just buttered a bee!

Songs of the Hidden Hollow

In the hollow, a party stirs the air,
A hedgehog with cupcakes shows he can share.
The birds join in with a chirpy tune,
While raccoons argue on who'll be the moon.

A carrot cake debate takes wild flight,
As the wise old owl tries to make it right.
Between the laughs, they dance around,
In the hidden hollows where joy can be found.

Beneath the Fronds of Time

Beneath the leaves, the critters play,
A squirrel juggles acorns all day.
The rabbit hops, with ears so high,
While butterflies giggle and fly by.

A hedgehog sneezes, what a surprise,
Causing frogs to leap with wide eyes.
The stumpy toad croaks a jest,
While ferns agree, they are quite the best.

Whispers on the Forest Floor

The ground tells tales, a ticklish breeze,
With mushrooms laughing beneath the trees.
A worm slides past, his dance quite grand,
While crickets form a quirky band.

An owl hoots jokes, a wise old soul,
As snails debate who's winning the race of role.
The dandelions smile at the fun,
While ants march on, their work never done.

The Soft Lament of Lichen

On rocks, the lichen sings a tune,
While slugs slide by, out for a swoon.
The mossy carpet, a giggling place,
Dance like no one's watching, what a space!

A sleepy cat naps, curled up tight,
Dreaming of fish, within the moonlight.
Mice plot pranks under the tree,
While owls chuckle at their glee.

Secrets of the Gnarled Branches

The old trees gossip, rustling leaves,
They share juicy tales, like sly thieves.
A squirrel's secret stash is found,
While raccoons laugh in the background sound.

A branch creaks softly, a ticklish scene,
As chipmunks tease, with faces so keen.
You'll never guess what the acorns said,
With secrets and laughter, they're never misled.

Murmurs of the Ancient Earth

Beneath the trees, a whispered joke,
A squirrel's laugh, a playful poke.
The roots dance secretly, in glee,
While ants march on, an army spree.

Old rocks chuckle, tales they tell,
Of windy days and mossy dwell.
The worms wiggle in a silly row,
While mushrooms giggle, 'Look at us grow!'

The breeze tickles leaves, a gentle tease,
Frogs croak laughter, buzzing with ease.
Echoes bounce from branch to stone,
In this green world, never alone.

So join this game, don't take a side,
In nature's humor, let's abide.
With every step, a jest you'll find,
A world that whispers, sweetly unconfined.

The Voice of the Untamed

In the wild, a rustling sound,
A raccoon grins, mischief abound.
The bushes giggle, swaying free,
As brambles tickle, just wait and see.

Birds squawk jokes from high up there,
While foxes dance without a care.
Toadstools nod, keeping the beat,
As crickets strum their tiny feet.

Gusts of wind, with chuckles mixed,
Sweeping past with clever tricks.
Nature's jesters, all around,
In the untamed air, laughter's found.

So take a stroll 'neath skies so vast,
Join the fun, forget the past.
For in this wild, a joyless strain,
Turns to giggles under the rain.

Dialogues with the Dappled Sunlight

Sunbeams peek through leafy shades,
Lighting up the dappled glades.
A butterfly whispers, 'What a show!'
While shadows giggle, putting on glow.

The flowers chatter in paisley hues,
Trading secrets, sharing views.
Their petals flutter, like tiny flags,
As bees buzz by with their zippy zags.

Each beam of light plays hide and seek,
Tickling the grass, a playful sneak.
Dancing down, the golden rays,
Prompting smiles for sweet summer days.

Join the banter, laugh it out,
Nature's bright voice is full of clout.
In sunlight's warmth, all worries cease,
In this bright romp, find your peace.

Unspoken Dreams in the Underwood

In the hush of leaves, dreams are shared,
Whispered wishes float through air.
A rabbit snickers, hoping to leap,
While shadows plot in a muddled heap.

The old oak chuckles, sensing the schemes,
While ferns giggle, lost in their dreams.
A hedgehog sighs, so wonderfully shy,
As the world spins on with a cheeky high.

Tiny fairies play hide and seek,
In the underwood, silliness peaks.
A glance from a deer, coy and sly,
Says, 'Join the fun, don't pass it by!'

So wander low where secrets bloom,
Dance with joy, let laughter consume.
In the realm of dreams, both wild and sweet,
Gather the moments, life can't be beat.

Gentle Voices on the Breeze

In the hush where the squirrels tease,
A rabbit hops with such great ease.
Leaves giggle as they brush by,
A dancing breeze, oh my oh my!

Frogs croak tales that make you grin,
They joke of flies and where they've been.
A chorus of chuckles rings out clear,
The woodlands laugh, it's plain, I fear!

Whispers twirl from tree to tree,
Telling tales of a bumblebee.
With every rustle and playful cheer,
The grove's a stand-up show, my dear!

As shadows play their silly tricks,
A woodpecker taps, what a quick fix!
Laughter spills beneath the sky,
In this wild place, we all comply!

Silence of the Wandering Sprites

Sprites float by with impish glee,
Whistling tunes of rhubarb tea.
In midair, they dance and spin,
Making laughter, a joyful din!

Pixies play hide and seek today,
In the wildflowers where children play.
Their giggles echo, so light and free,
Telling tales of what should never be!

As shadows stretch under the sun's might,
A gnome trips over, what a sight!
The sprites just burst into joyful cheer,
While he grumbles, all red and clear!

In the silence of their fairy realm,
They're plotting mischief at the helm.
Giggles drift on warming air,
Mischief blooms, no need for a care!

Reflections in the Dew-Kissed Air

Dewdrops wink in the soft first light,
Fireflies twinkle, a wondrous sight.
They flash their jokes in a dazzling dance,
In the flittering glow, who wouldn't prance?

A sleepy owl hoots, "What's the plan?"
While a busy ant drags a crumb, how grand!
The morning glimmers, laughter bright,
In leafy depths, fun takes flight!

Breezes carry whispers sweet and airy,
As mushrooms giggle, oh so merry.
Dew-kissed leaves join in the cheer,
It's a raucous party, let's all veer!

And when the sun starts rising high,
A chipmunk chuckles with a sigh.
"Why not dance till day's end?" they cheer,
In this haven, there's no fear!

The Poetry of the Shade

Under branches that twist and sway,
Nature spills rhymes, come what may.
The sunbeams giggle, play their part,
With shadows that dance in merry art.

A sleeping bear snores with delight,
While fireflies paint the coming night.
Winks and nudges from the trees,
All share secrets on the gentle breeze.

In this realm of kinship so bold,
Gossip travels as the tales unfold.
The rabbits chuckle, squirrels debate,
In the shade, it's never too late!

And on a dare, a toad sings loud,
Surrounded by an enthusiastic crowd.
The poetry flows, it's quite a charade,
In the laughter of the leafy glade!

Footprints in the Ferny Shadows

In shadows deep where ferns grow tall,
A squirrel giggles, causing a sprawl.
He trips on roots, what a sight to see,
Chasing his tail, nearly spills his tea.

The rabbits whisper, a secret of speed,
They hop over logs, fulfill their greed.
A dance in the dusk, with twirls and hops,
The deer just chuckle, while munching on crops.

Funky little crickets, with legs that snap,
Host an odd concert in twilight's lap.
The owls roll their eyes, in wise old delight,
As the forest livens under the moonlight.

So here in the grove, let laughter resound,
With every footstep, joy's easily found.
A merry mishap in nature's own way,
Sprinkling humor upon the green play.

The Quiet Euphony of the Wild

Whispers of winds play through the leaves,
A raccoon hums, while no one believes.
He juggles acorns, how clumsy he is,
The bandit's a fool, but he thinks he's a whiz.

Twinkling stars watch over the scene,
As hedgehogs roll, covered in green.
They tumble and fumble without a care,
While fireflies chuckle, lighting the air.

Branches sway gently, a soft serenade,
The frogs join in, not one is afraid.
They croak and they chirp, some off-key at best,
But it's all just a part of nature's quest.

So dance to the tunes that the forest arranges,
With giggles and grins, nature exchanges.
In the quiet of night, let joy be unfurled,
Where the echoes are funny, just like the world.

Secrets Tucked in the Bark

Amongst the trees, where the whispers thrive,
A woodpecker taps, trying to survive.
He tells tall tales of bugs that he found,
With each little knock, new stories abound.

A snail in a shell, slow as can be,
Dreams of a race with the bumblebee.
They chuckle and plot, who'll win in the end?
While the ants all cheer, oh what a blend!

The mushrooms share gossip, so juicy and ripe,
About the young sprouts and their silly type.
They giggle and wiggle in damp earthy cheer,
While a shy little beetle listens near.

So delve into secrets that nature shares,
With laughter and glee, strip off all cares.
For amongst all the bark, if you look with your heart,
You'll find funny tales—what a wild art!

Cadences of the Canopied Silence

Under the boughs where the sunbeams play,
A cat sneaks past, in a stealthy ballet.
He leaps on a log, miscalculates the jump,
And lands in a puddle—what a delightful clump!

A butterfly flutters, dressed in bright hues,
Teasing a beetle with silly old blues.
They dance in a circle, a whimsical chase,
Around the tall grasses, in a beautiful race.

The toads hold a meeting, in a swampy disguise,
Debating the merits of flies and of pies.
With croaks and with croons, they quibble and jest,
While the dragonflies glide, at life's merry fest.

So tread softly here, where the humor ignites,
In the still of the woods, under starry nights.
For the secret of laughter in nature's grand scheme,
Is found in the silliness—oh, what a dream!

The Silk of Sunlit Secrets

In a glade where shadows creep,
A squirrel stirs from its deep sleep,
With acorns piled high, what a sight,
Pretending to guard them with all its might.

The sun plays tricks, in beams it spins,
Dancing dust where the mischief begins,
A rabbit giggles, a deer turns red,
As they swap tales of what they've said.

A chipmunk jumps with a cheeky grin,
Claiming the prize for fastest twin,
But the turtle just laughs, slow and sage,
Winning by patience, not by wage.

In this grove of secrets and jest,
Where every creature's oddly blessed,
With a wink and a hop, they play their part,
Nature's comedy springs from the heart.

Awareness in the Woodland Veil

A fox in glasses takes a peek,
Scribbling notes as the others squeak,
'Why are you dressed in plaid today?'
The wise old owl just rolls away.

Parrots chatter, who's heard the latest?
The raccoon claims he's the greatest,
'But your mask is crooked, friend,' they tease,
As he strikes a pose with grace and ease.

Underneath a toadstool, ants parade,
Carrying crumbs like a grand charade,
While fireflies blink in constant cheer,
Offering light to those who draw near.

In the twilight, laughter fills the air,
As nature's cast performs with flair,
Each creature's folly, their unique song,
In this veil, nothing feels wrong.

The Symphony of Swaying Branches

The trees stretch high, a leafy stage,
Where squirrels act in a nutty craze,
They bounce and leap with joyous squeals,
While the branches clap like enthusiastic heels.

A woodpecker drums a silly beat,
As critters gather for this treat,
With chipmunks breaking into a dance,
In nature's glen, everyone takes a chance.

Each rustle and shake, a cue for fun,
As mushrooms groove under the sun,
The breeze carries tunes, soft and clear,
While the pinecone jokes bring everyone near.

Together they sway, a sight to behold,
In nature's rhythm, both brave and bold,
In this symphony of leafy cheer,
Laughter echoes, so loud and clear.

The Dance of Decomposing Leaves

Fallen leaves swirl like happy ghosts,
In colors bright, they gather in flocks,
'Watch my twirl!' calls a leaf with flair,
But a gopher scoffs, 'I'll beat you there!'

The wind hums low, a cheeky song,
As critters join in, all dancing along,
'Let's have a race!' cries a sprightly twig,
While a snail giggles, quite shy and big.

Worms wriggle through the musty floor,
Tickling toes, oh what a chore,
With laughter echoing in the trees,
And the essence of humor carried with ease.

A patch of moss holds the joyful scene,
With laughter wrapped in emerald green,
As creatures celebrate, so wild, so free,
In the dance of leaves, pure jubilee.

Stories Woven by the Wind

In the woods where the tall trees sway,
A squirrel chases shadows all day.
With acorns flying, he makes a fuss,
Declaring war on the nearby bus.

Leaves giggle with whispers and tales,
About a turtle who dreams of sails.
His tiny boat made from a leaf,
He sails the stream, oh what a belief!

A rabbit builds castles from twigs,
Dreaming of weather, and fancy digs.
But a sly fox says, with a gleeful grin,
"Your royal throne is where I dive in!"

So the wind weaves laughter and cheer,
In a place where no one sheds a tear.
With each little squeak, a story's spun,
In this forest, oh joy—what fun!

Reverberations from the Roots

Deep down where the whispers meet,
The roots are dancing, oh what a feat!
They tickle the worms with glee and cheer,
Proclaiming, "We're the life of the year!"

A bushy raccoon, clad in a bow tie,
Tells knock-knock jokes while passing by.
He juggles the mushrooms, a sight to behold,
As laughter echoes, stories unfold.

The grass hums tunes, oh so sublime,
While flowers sway to the rhythm and rhyme.
A beetle performs with a tap and a slide,
Beneath a broad leaf, where secrets hide.

In the tapestry sewn with roots and laughter,
Nature plots joy—what comes after?
A symphony spun in playful delight,
In this oddball world, every day's bright!

The Stillness Between the Pines

Amidst tall pines, the stillness brews,
A chipmunk in socks reads the news.
"Did you hear about the squirrel's great hair?"
"His fluffy style's beyond compare!"

The breeze delivers secrets in twirls,
As butterflies gossip and whirl.
"Did you see the frog in a jacket so neat?
He's jumped into fashion—what a treat!"

A crow croons softly, wearing a hat,
While a lizard debates if it's too warm for that.
So beneath pines, the laughter takes flight,
With stories that echo from morning till night.

Tickled by shadows, light dances too,
In this world, there's always something new.
Each rustle and giggle takes center stage,
As nature scripts joy on her vibrant page!

Chronicles of the Verdant Realm

In a realm where the breezes spin,
A hedgehog's zany dance starts to begin.
"Step right up! Witness this show,"
As bugs applaud from the front row.

A wise old owl, with spectacles worn,
Cracks jokes about the day he was born.
His hoots echo, shaking the leaves,
While laughter flits through like playful thieves.

The flowers plot mischief, all bright and bold,
Telling tales of the shy seeds they hold.
While daisies make crowns of the sun's sweet rays,
Petals burst forth with their own wild plays.

In the verdant realm, joy always swells,
Where whimsy and laughter cast magical spells.
So come join the fun in this leafy space,
Where every moment's a grin on a face!

Serenade of the Shaded Sanctuary

In a nook where shadows play,
A squirrel steals the show today.
Chasing his tail with fervent glee,
He nearly trips on a sleepy bee.

A parrot squawks with cheeky flair,
Telling jokes of the old oak's hair.
The leaves giggle, a rustling sound,
As laughter dances all around.

A chipmunk dons a tiny hat,
While the rabbits cheer, 'Oh, look at that!'
A parade of critters, wild and free,
In this funny grove of harmony.

As dusk arrives, the fireflies wink,
They sway and twirl, as if to think.
In this shaded haven, joy takes flight,
Nature's comedy, a pure delight.

The Language of Living Roots

Deep below, where secrets twitch,
The roots speak softly, a giddy pitch.
A worm pipes up with a pun so slick,
While mushrooms giggle, their sides they'll lick.

The badgers ponder life's great quest,
With riddles posed, they pass the test.
The moss nods warm, a fuzzy friend,
As laughter echoes, around it bends.

A raccoon dons a monocle grand,
Cracking jokes, a one-cool band.
The trees join in, with creaks and sways,
In this lively chat, the world displays.

Underneath, where roots align,
A comedy show, so divine.
Nature's humor—a lively spree,
In this underground jubilee.

Dialogues with the Dappled Light

The sunlight chuckles through the leaves,
Tickling the grass that softly heaves.
A butterfly spins, a dance so spry,
With a wink and a twirl, off it will fly.

A wise old owl clears his throat,
As patchy sunlight takes a gloat,
'Why did the chicken cross the glen?'
The animals roar, 'To join us again!'

A playful breeze sends whispers round,
With stories of pranks from the forest ground.
A rabbit faints in exaggerated flair,
While the deer just rolls their eyes in despair.

In dappled light, the laughter threads,
With tales of the forest, where joy spreads.
Each ray a comedian, lighting the way,
In this harmonious, funny ballet.

The Soliloquy of Starlit Branches

Under stars that twinkle bright,
The branches chatter, a funny sight.
'Have you seen that raccoon tonight?'
'He danced with the moon! What a delight!'

The owls hoot in perfect tune,
As shadows bounce with the glowing moon.
A fox tells tales of the day gone by,
While the fireflies burst with a giggly sigh.

The branches sway, a subtle dance,
While whispers of humor take their chance.
A shoot so brave, it sings aloud,
Joining the chorus of a lively crowd.

In the quiet night, the laughter thrives,
Nature's jesters, the world revives.
So here beneath the celestial waltz,
The trees find joy; who needs impromptu sals?

Soft Footfalls on the Forest Floor

In the woods where squirrels chat,
A raccoon wears a top hat.
Frogs join in with a croaky tune,
Dance around under the moon.

Mice parade in their tiny shoes,
As crickets boast of their best moves.
Every twig snaps like a joke,
Trees laugh in the breeze, they spoke.

Beneath each leaf, a prank unfolds,
Nature's laughter, pure and bold.
With every rustle, a giggle grows,
The forest floor knows all our woes.

So come along, join the spree,
Nature's jesters, you and me.
With soft footfalls, let's explore,
And leave our worries at the door.

Reflections in the Quiet Grove

In stillness, a squirrel tells a tale,
About a snail that lost its trail.
The birds chuckle at the delay,
As butterflies join in the play.

A bashful hedgehog starts to prance,
Forgets its worries, joins the dance.
The shadows giggle, twist, and twine,
As sunlight winks in a straight line.

With whispers soft, the leaves tease,
A frog hops high, then lands with ease.
Laughter echoes through every grove,
Nature's antics, the heart will strove.

Come join the fun, don't be shy,
The trees will cheer, the clouds will fly.
In each reflection, joy is found,
In the quiet, humor abounds.

Murmuring Willows by the Stream

By the stream where willows sway,
Fish tell tales of their brave day.
A duck quacks loud, with flair and grace,
While frogs laugh, hopping in place.

The water sparkles, winks in glee,
As turtles plot and giggle with me.
Dragonflies buzz, making a fuss,
A dance-off starts—who's got the plus?

The willows whisper to the breeze,
Inviting all to share their ease.
With splashes and swishes, fun they weave,
In the heart of the green, we believe.

So grab your friend, leap and shout,
In this joyful place, there's no doubt.
With murmuring laughs around every bend,
Nature's rib-tickles never end.

The Chorus of Ancient Trees

In a circle, the tall ones stand,
Spouting jokes, so unplanned.
Boughs sway gently, a rhythm divine,
Their laughter blends like sweet, sweet wine.

With roots that shuffle, leaves that sway,
They share puns in an ancient way.
Two owls hoot, a comical pair,
In the chorus, they flair and share.

A chubby fox rolls, a sight so rare,
While a wise old crow watches with care.
Each tree's quirk adds to the tune,
As laughter spills beneath the moon.

So visit the grove, take a seat,
Join in the fun, feel the beat.
With the chorus of trees, let joy soar,
In nature's laugh, we want more.

Enchanted Overgrowth

In the forest where giggles grow,
Squirrels dance with a wobbly flow.
Mushrooms wear hats of silly glee,
Whispering secrets to the bumblebee.

A rabbit with glasses reads a map,
While owls in cloaks take a midday nap.
The flowers chuckle, a comical sight,
As butterflies flutter with pure delight.

Frogs play cards beneath the shade,
While lizards in coats come out to parade.
Each crack in the earth shares a funny tale,
As the breezes giggle and the branches sail.

So if you wander through this green spree,
Join the laughter, feel the glee.
For in this patch of leafy jokes,
Every creature's laughter gently pokes.

Flickers of Sunlit Silence

Sunbeams tickle the leaves above,
While critters gather to share their love.
A squirrel with sass juggles acorns wide,
As the sunbeams dance, they all take pride.

A bear in shades swings to a funky beat,
While bees in tuxedos buzz and tweet.
In the dappled light, shadows prance,
And flowers sway as if in a dance.

Chirping crickets hold a comedy show,
With punchlines so wild, it's hard to know.
The tall grass tickles a skunk with cheer,
And together they laugh, not sparking fear.

In this flickering glow, the humor flows,
As nature's quirks put on grandiose shows.
So pause and listen to the fun all around,
In quiet moments, joy can be found.

The Language of the Trees

In leafy whispers, the oaks convey,
Stories of squirrels, cats and their play.
Pine trees giggle, shaking their tops,
While willows sway with soft, leafy flops.

A wise old elm tells jokes of yore,
While maples chuckle, wanting more.
Chipmunks translate with a rapid fire,
As petals flutter, adding to the choir.

Branches bend low to catch the glee,
Each rustle of leaves sings harmony.
They gossip of sunlight and playful rain,
In the vast canopy, jokes remain.

So listen closely as you roam through,
The symphony of laughter in shades of hue.
In the language of the trees, joy's the call,
United in humor, they enchant us all.

Soliloquy of the Hidden Path

On the winding trail where secrets bloom,
A snail throws a party with laughter and room.
Worms in tuxedos do the cha-cha slide,
While mushrooms giggle, all spruced up with pride.

A hedgehog wearing a tiny bowtie,
Serves up stories to passersby.
Crickets crack jokes as the sun dips low,
Creating a scene that steals the show.

Between the ferns, the shadows play,
Making silly faces at the end of the day.
The path, a comedian, twists and bends,
As each little creature brings joy to their friends.

So take a step down this whimsical lane,
Join the antics, share in the gain.
For in this hidden path that we roam,
Laughter and joy create a true home.

Lullabies of the Leafy Glade

In the glade where leaves tickle,
Frogs croak out a silly giggle.
Squirrels dance in their puffy pants,
While twigs snap like a funny chance.

Crickets strum a playful tune,
Under the watch of the silver moon.
Butterflies prance with silly grace,
Making faces in their vibrant race.

The breezes whisper quirky jokes,
As mushrooms wear their hats like folks.
All around, the laughter spins,
In nature's game, nobody wins!

So come and join this rustic cheer,
Amidst the trees, with friends sincere.
A leafy lullaby, strong and bold,
Where laughter's tales are often told.

Enigmas of the Moss-Covered Path

On a path where the shadows play,
A raccoon teaches kids ballet.
Mossy slippers dance with glee,
As squirrels giggle, 'Just wait for me!'

A whispering wind twirls jokes anew,
While hedgehogs share a riddle or two.
The trees can't hold their giggling charms,
As rabbits flaunt their tiny arms.

Curious foxes, a puzzling crew,
Chase their tails like they always do.
Each twist and turn a silly sight,
In the woods where wrong feels right.

Here, enigmas make the heart feel light,
A riddle's punchline takes flight.
With laughter echoing all around,
In this merry path, joy is found.

Rustling Reveries in the Greenery

In the thicket, leaves play tag,
While toads in tune sing like a rag.
Giggling branches, they wiggle about,
Echoing giggles, there's never a doubt.

A squirrel wears a cap of pine,
Claiming it's a fashion divine.
While beetles wear shoes so bright,
Finding partners for a dance tonight.

The daisies gossip, spread the word,
About a hummingbird's silly absurd.
With every rustle and sparkling beam,
Nature plots its next wacky dream.

So wander here and join the scene,
Where every glance holds laughter keen.
In this rustling grove of delight,
Fun and folly dance through the night.

Sighs of the Twilight Thicket

Under the twilight's tippy toes,
The owls ponder silly woes.
With glasses perched on their beaks,
They read the branches; oh, the freaks!

The hedgehog wears a little frown,
Complains about his spiky crown.
Meanwhile, turtles speed like a race,
Chasing shadows, a funny chase.

Crickets chirp with a laugh so bright,
Tickled pink by firefly light.
Each moment's a comic splash,
In the thicket, we all dash.

So join the sighs of glee and jest,
In the twilight thicket, we are blessed.
With laughter floating in the air,
This charming place, beyond compare!

Echoes Among the Ferns

In the glade, a squirrel pranced,
Chasing shadows, how he danced!
A raccoon laughed, with mischief bright,
'Twas just a game, oh what a sight!

The owl blinked with rolling eyes,
As crickets chirped their little lies.
'You're the king of silly things!'
The forest giggled, as fun it brings.

A frog in boots jumped with glee,
'Look at me! I'm fancy-free!'
The flowers chuckled, swaying slow,
'That frog's a star at this show!'

Each rustle, every little sound,
Comedic tales that swirl around.
In nature's laugh, joy does thrive,
A party's where the fun's alive!

Songs of the Sylvan Shadows

Beneath the shade, a fox did croon,
Wearing glasses, quite the buffoon.
A rabbit joined, with carrot flares,
Together they sang without cares.

The trees swayed with a rhythmic beat,
As acorns rolled beneath their feet.
Chirps of birds made a silly tune,
'Join us now, it's time to swoon!'

A deer tried dancing on two toes,
Stumbling over branches, oh how it goes!
With laughter echoing through the wood,
In every heart, the cheer was good.

And when the sun began to set,
The nighttime critters sang with zest.
A chorus formed beneath the moon,
'It's the woodland party, join us soon!'

Hushed Tales of the Woodland

Tucked between the mossy trees,
A snail did tell of his slow squeeze.
'I'm racing fast!' he said with pride,
As a ladybug laughed, quite wide.

The mushroom cap wore a goofy hat,
While a beetle joined to dance and chat.
'This is the best, oh what a thrill!'
With each new tale, time stood still.

The winds carried giggles on their wings,
As owls mocked the most silly things.
'Whooo's the best at making fun?'
The forest laughed as one by one.

In every nook, the jests parade,
With each sweet moment, a joke is made.
So come my friends, bring smiles with glee,
In this woodland, forever carefree!

Breezes Through the Undergrowth

A breezy laugh swept through the ferns,
Where a playful mouse took turns.
With tiny shoes, it twirled about,
Chasing shadows with a joyful shout.

Behind a bush, a badger snored,
While a hedgehog on a skateboard roared.
'Can you believe my fast new ride?'
Underneath the branches, filled with pride.

The wind whistled tunes like a silly clown,
Tickling leaves as it danced around.
And when the dusk began to fall,
The woodland critters had a ball.

So laugh with me, in nature's embrace,
Where fun and folly freely race.
With every rustle, every breeze,
The world outside just fades with ease.

Secrets in the Sunlit Shroud

In the glade where shadows play,
Squirrels gossip all the day.
With acorns flying, giggles soar,
Who knew trees could want for more?

Frogs in boots make quite a scene,
Dancing wildly, oh so keen.
Grasshoppers join in the fun,
As the sun sets, they just run!

A rabbit speaks in riddles vague,
While crickets laugh in leafy plague.
Breezes tease and tickle the bark,
Under branches, they leave their mark.

With each rustle, a prank unfolds,
Tiny tales the forest holds.
Laughter echoes in the light,
Nature's jesters, pure delight!

Whispers of Wildflowers at Dusk

Petals giggle in the breeze,
Tickling bulbs with such great ease.
Bees just buzz their silly song,
Joining in where they belong.

A daisy winks at clover's plight,
'You're too short to fly tonight!'
Butterflies flap with style so grand,
'Look at me, I'm so unplanned!'

As twilight falls, the colors swirl,
With a dance, each bloom will twirl.
No worries in this garden space,
Every flower knows their place.

Under stars, the laughter grows,
Echoing joy wherever it flows.
In this patch, they play till dawn,
Wildflowers flirt, then carries on!

The Sounds of Serenity Among the Ferns

Ferns whisper secrets soft and light,
Tickling noses in the night.
Toadstools giggle, taking turns,
As each new tale of mischief burns.

A snail named Fred paints on a wall,
Says, 'I'm busy – have a ball!'
The owls hoot in jestful fright,
'Is it day? Or just a light?'

A hedgehog struts in funky shoes,
Twirling 'round with happy blues.
While beetles dance, all fancy and bold,
In this grove, such stories told.

Nighttime holds a carnival vibe,
Where frenzied fun is the tribe.
In shadows deep, the laughter swells,
Among the ferns, each story tells!

Echoing Dreams of the Woodland Spirits

'Tis said the spirits play by night,
With bouncing balls, oh what a sight!
They tickle branches, throw a show,
In moonlit clearings, voices flow.

A raccoon juggles shiny stones,
While owlets giggle, in soft tones.
With twinkling eyes, the shadows sway,
Dancing sprites in a game of play.

The wind whispers each secret shared,
As grass blades sway, slightly bared.
Laughter rings from every tree,
In this place where spirits be.

As dawn approaches, echoes fade,
Yet threads of joy are deftly laid.
With every rustle, hearts entwine,
In the woodland, laughter divine!

Tales Spun by Twilight Breezes

In twilight's clutch a squirrel doth prance,
He wears a hat, oh what a chance!
His acorn stash, quite finely kept,
Yet on the ground, he often slept.

The rabbits giggle as shadows flit,
They play at cards, their wits a hit.
With leafy hats and sticks for cues,
They wager carrots, oh what a ruse!

But through the trees, a gusty shout,
A chipmunk bold, there's no doubt!
"Who stole my snacks?" he cries aloud,
A dancing crowd, both brave and proud.

As stars peek in, the night's a stage,
With critters up, the laughter's wage.
In jest and glee, the tales expand,
In twilight's glow, this merry band.

Lingering Sentiments of the Leafy Refuge

A porcupine with quills so fine,
Claims his throne, saying, "This is mine!"
Yet a hare hops by, with mischief laid,
"Those prickly things? A silly trade!"

The turtles tell of grass so sweet,
They wager who can find a treat.
One munches clover, another a sprout,
"Can you beat me?" they laugh and shout.

A wise old owl roosts high in the fray,
"Stop your bickering, just eat and play!"
Yet no one hears as they scurry by,
The wisdom lost in raucous sighs.

With every rustle and laughter shared,
The leafy refuge becomes a fair!
In silly squabbles and feathery fun,
The day's mischief has only begun.

Whispers Beneath the Canopy

Amidst the greens, a frog does croak,
He claims a throne, all jest and joke.
With flies for guests, he throws a ball,
"Jump if you dare, I'll catch them all!"

The beetles dance in pairs, so spry,
They glide about, they twist and fly.
"Oh, what a night!" the fireflies gleam,
Their lights a flick'ry, dreamy beam.

The hedgehogs snicker at the game,
With prickly backs, they take no blame.
As friends convene beneath moonlight,
Their laughter echoes into the night.

With leafy whispers, tales unfold,
Of tiny antics brave and bold.
In this embrace, the night ignites,
In joy and jest, beneath the lights.

Secrets of the Leafy Labyrinth

In winding paths where shadows creep,
A tiny mouse has secrets to keep.
He hid his cheese where no one peeks,
Now laughs and jests spill out in squeaks.

Two owls bicker, "Who's wiser here?"
Their hoots of pride will never clear.
"Your hooting's flat, you've lost your tone,"
"Then speak for me, while I sit alone!"

A hedgehog rolls into the fray,
"Let's settle this, no more delay!"
With spiky grace, he starts a dance,
"Join in or go, don't miss your chance!"

As twilight dims, the leaf-strewn ground,
Brings laughter out, a joyous sound.
In secret realms where folly grows,
The leafy maze, where silliness flows.

The Soft Footfall of Nature

In the glen where shadows play,
Squirrels dance with nuts in sway.
The owls hoot out a quirky tune,
As rabbits plot beneath the moon.

Frogs debate on lily pads,
While hedgehogs sport their funky fads.
A raccoon flips through treasure chests,
Finding snacks on nature's quests.

Melodies Between the Moss and Stone

A chipmunk chirps a silly joke,
While fireflies in the dark provoke.
The stones chuckle, they seem to know,
Of gnomes that trip on roots and grow.

Beneath the boughs, a picnic's spread,
With sandwiches meant for someone's head.
The wind hums sweet, with cheeky flair,
As daisies wink without a care.

Enigmas of the Flora Envelop

The daisies gossip, oh what a sight,
While mushrooms giggle in the twilight.
A some fox tries to wear a hat,
But, oh dear, it flops — he looks a brat.

Worms in the soil compose a band,
With rhythm set by nature's hand.
The willows sway, their secrets kept,
As ants march by, all well-prepped.

Tales of the Gentle Glade

In the clearing, a tall tale spins,
Where toads debate on who wins.
The trees lean in to hear the fun,
And giggle softly at the pun.

The brook babbles with witty charm,
Splashing a fish, who means no harm.
With every quip the world grows bright,
In the glade, all worries take flight.

Tales from the Hollowed Trunks

In the hollow trunk, a cricket sings,
A tale of cheese for the forest kings.
The owl chuckles, a wise old sage,
As the squirrels dance on the mossy stage.

Raccoons conspire with crafty names,
While the old oak blames it on the games.
Each bark whispers jokes, the laughter flows,
As the sun peeks through where nobody goes.

A hedgehog in a hat, a sight so rare,
Jumps in puddles without a care.
He winks at the fawn with mischief bright,
A splash of mud is the best delight!

The night rolls in, with fireflies cheer,
Telling stories for all who hear.
Each shadow dances, each root has fun,
In the grove, every day is a pun.

The Enigma of the Mossy Veil

Behind the veil, a gossip spreads,
A squirrel stealing from the flower beds.
The toadstools giggle, vibrating low,
As ants march in a grand parade show.

Where the shadows twirl and giggles fly,
A chipmunk grins with a curious eye.
He's hiding nuts while crafting a tale,
In the secret space beneath the pale.

A wise old turtle in a top hat waits,
For the laughter to dance through the forest gates.
With a wink and a nod, he joins the scene,
In the enigma where nothing's routine.

Night crickets croon with a comedic flair,
As the moon sneaks in like it's unaware.
The chatter grows loud, like an echoing choir,
In this quirky place, laughter won't tire.

Spirit Songs of the Underbrush

In the darkened brush, soft giggles rise,
A raccoon wearing grandma's old disguise.
The rabbits chime in with their flute-like squeals,
While the hedgehogs plot their prickly appeals.

With a rustle and tumble, the bushes gossip,
As the moon beams down, no one can stop it.
The owls hold court, their laughter rings,
Echoing through as the nightingale sings.

A lizard in shades basking in style,
Says, "Every slip is just part of the smile."
Twirling around with a flamboyant flair,
Leaves rustle softly, who's dancing there?

The spirits of fun swirl the night air,
In the underbrush where joy's everywhere.
The whispers of mirth, they bounce with glee,
In this leafy realm, it's all jubilee.

The Serenity of Subtle Sounds

Whispers of laughter ride on the breeze,
As the beetle breaks bricks, taking it with ease.
Fluffy clouds chuckle, drifting away,
As the sunlight creates a comic ballet.

The ferns join in, swaying side to side,
Their leafy humor, they just can't hide.
A hummingbird zips with a giggle so sweet,
While the dandelions compete in retreat.

A wise old spider spins tales in silk,
His web is adorned with the milk of the ilk.
Laughter overflows as crickets confide,
In this forest haven where joy won't subside.

Each rustle and ripple, a soft serenade,
Crafting memories in nature's parade.
In the heart of the grove, where humor abounds,
Life's a quirky jest in subtle sounds.

Intimate Conversations in the Canopy

In the trees, a chatty squirrel,
Stashes acorns with a twirl.
He'll tell you all the woodland jokes,
While dodging clumsy, laughing folks.

The leaves above, they shake and sway,
A gossiping breeze that joins the play.
"Did you hear about the feisty crow?
Her dance moves are all the rage, you know!"

Underneath, a rabbit prances,
Wearing tiny shoes for chances.
He hops and skips, with flair and glee,
"Join me in this leap, it's free!"

And thus unfolds a sunny day,
Amidst the laughter and the fray.
For in the grove, with joy we boast,
Amidst the chatter, we play the host.

Breath of the Wildflower Whisper

A bumblebee sings a gentle tune,
Buzzing softly, morning's boon.
"Ever tried to dance on a flower?
It's all the rage, swing with power!"

The daisies blush as winds pass by,
Hiding giggles, oh my, oh my!
With petals waving, they poke and tease,
"Watch your steps, give us some ease!"

A butterfly flutters with flair,
Chasing shadows in midair.
"Is it me, or is that a joke
About the snail dressed as a bloke?"

And in the field, laughter ignites,
With whimsical tales that take flight.
Each bloom shares stories in soft whispers,
Covering all the forest's twisters.

The Veil of Soft Petals

Underneath a drooping bloom,
A ladybug plays a tune.
With tiny feet, she taps away,
Saying, "Life's a game, let's play!"

The petals giggle, swaying light,
"Why did the grass refuse to fight?"
A nearby fern chuckles and sways,
"Because it knew it would be hay!"

In shadows cast by softest leaves,
A wily fox in trickery weaves.
"Who's the best at hide and seek?
Not me, I'm here—but don't peek!"

And laughter dances on the breeze,
With every rustle, all at ease.
For beneath this vibrant cover,
Every creature finds a brother.

Rhythms of the Resilient Thicket

In a thicket, snickers soar,
As frogs croak loudly, wanting more.
"Did you hear? It's epic news!
The pond has lost its wayward hues!"

A hedgehog rolls, a ball of fun,
Inviting all for a quick run.
"Catch me if you can, let's spin,
But watch your back, I've got my kin!"

Bouncing berries laugh and sigh,
With faces bright against the sky.
"Join the ruckus, bring your cheer,
In this vibrant grove, we persevere!"

With each rustle and playful shout,
Lively spirits dance about.
For in this cozy, green-locked space,
Every joke finds a happy place.

Memories of the Glistening Glade

In the glade where laughter floats,
A squirrel wears a tiny coat.
He twirls and spins, quite the sight,
Dancing under the moonlight.

Frogs croak jokes, a comic troupe,
While rabbits form a silly loop.
They hop and skip on foliage green,
The funniest creatures you've ever seen.

A breeze plays tricks, it tickles leaves,
The trees dance too, oh how they weave!
In this place where joy collides,
Nature giggles and never hides.

So laugh aloud, come join the fun,
In the glade where antics run.
A place where whimsy's on the rise,
Where even mushrooms wear disguise.

The Heartbeat of Hidden Springs

At hidden springs where fish can grin,
A cat invents new fun to spin.
He wears a hat, slightly askew,
As wise old owls hoot, 'How do you do?'

The turtles race on lily pads,
With the quickness of determined lads.
They slip and slide, a raucous cheer,
Even the rocks crack jokes, oh dear!

The frogs debate, who jumps the best,
With splashes flying, they're quite obsessed.
A chorus of croaks fills the air,
While beavers build, unaware of their fare.

So heed the springs, where laughter flows,
And life's a stage, where everyone glows.
In hidden realms of joy and jest,
Nature's humor knows no rest.

Elysian Echoes of the Grove

In gleeful echoes, the trees conspire,
With whispers of jokes to lift you higher.
The flowers chuckle, petals aglow,
At the antics happening down below.

A hedgehog's quill, it pokes like a pen,
As he writes stories of critters and men.
A dance-off ensues, who can win?
The fox's grin shows he's all in!

The brook giggles at paw-print trails,
While butterflies tell the silliest tales.
From acorns to cacti, all join the throng,
In a forest where everyone sings along.

So tiptoe 'neath the branches that sway,
Join the whimsy of each playful day.
For in this grove, where laughter's a rite,
Every mishap is pure delight!

Tranquil Revelations of the Thicket

In the thicket where secrets play,
The rabbits gossip all day.
With twinkling eyes and twitching nose,
They share tales only nature knows.

The badger tells of his grandest feat,
Of evading the fox with light on his feet.
The birds exchange quips, so cheeky and bright,
Their verses sprout wings, taking flight.

A chipmunk races for his own acorn,
He slips and slides, oh bless, he's torn!
Laughter erupts, it fills the air,
As he puffs and huffs without a care.

So wander through this thicket divine,
Find joy in each curve, every intertwine.
For in the wild where laughter reigns,
Even the simple leaves hold gains.

Conversations with the Celestial Canopy

The leaves are laughing high above,
Telling secrets, just like a dove.
The branches dance like silly sprites,
Whispering jokes on starry nights.

A squirrel chimes in with a tease,
Climbing high among the trees.
An owl hoots a punchline neat,
While moonlit shadows tap their feet.

The clouds reply in puffy huffs,
As fireflies share their twinkling stuff.
Each rustle comes with giggle fits,
In this place where nonsense sits.

Oh, Celestial friends so spry,
Chit-chatting 'neath the twilight sky.
In the Grove where laughter flows,
Every leaf a comedic prose.

The Pulse of the Flourishing Underworld

Beneath the ground, where fungi grow,
The critters plot a stand-up show.
Worms wriggle in uproarious fads,
Crickets pop jokes that make them glad.

A toad croaks out a joke or two,
While moles wear hats—who knew?
The roots are tangled in a dance,
Poking fun at their own prance.

The fungi giggle with caps aloft,
While beetles roll their eyes, quite soft.
Each echo carries a chuckle tune,
In this realm where humor blooms.

Joy sprouts up from every thrum,
In a world where laughter's never glum.
The underworld pulses with glee,
A comedy show for all to see.

Dreams Within the Green Tapestry

In a quilt of leaves, thoughts take flight,
Where insects dream through the velvet night.
A butterfly tells of a big parade,
While crickets croon in the leafy shade.

The flowers snicker, their petals wide,
As vines play tag, the bugs they hide.
A snail giggles, slow and sly,
Underneath a mushroom, oh so high.

Winds scatter whispers of silly schemes,
While frogs play croquet on moonlit beams.
Every rustle tells a humorous tale,
In this land where jests never pale.

So come take a dream in this verdant calm,
Where laughter's the ultimate charm.
In the green tapestry, joy's unspun,
Each nightfall blossoms with whimsical fun.

Echoes of Lost Footsteps

In the hush of the grove, we hear a tread,
Footprints trailing laughter instead.
Boots bounce along with a playful song,
Chasing shadows where they belong.

A pair of socks has lost its way,
Telling stories of grand dismay.
While sneakers giggle, a sneaky pair,
Two left shoes, oh, what a rare affair!

The ground remembers each clumsy glide,
As echoes tickle and gently chide.
Every stumble, a reason to cheer,
For silly struts bring us all near.

So heed the path where footprints stray,
With a wink of joy along the way.
In the grove where laughter leads,
Every lost step plants laughter's seeds.

Whispers of the Wandering Breeze

In the grove where the wild things play,
A squirrel sings his quirky way,
With acorns dancing in the air,
He prances with a carefree flair.

A breeze sneezes, a leaf takes flight,
Tickling noses, oh what a sight!
The trees chuckle, branches bend low,
As critters join the merry show.

Bumblebees buzz with a bop and a roll,
Stumbling over their sweet honey goal,
While birds flirt with the notes they hum,
A symphony of nature, oh so fun!

Even the rocks in their stone-cold ways,
Giggle softly on sunlit days,
As shadows chase the paths they roam,
In this lively, mossy home.

Serenades in the Stillness

A toad croaks a croaky tune,
Beneath the watchful, grinning moon,
With every note, he sweeps through grass,
While fireflies twinkle, oh what a class!

The owl hoots with a wise old laugh,
As crickets join in, a musical staff,
The breeze whispers secrets, light and bright,
While shadows teeter, lost in delight.

Rabbits hop, with a skip and a slide,
Chasing their tails, with laughter as guide,
In this quiet place, hilarity thrives,
As senses awaken, each spirit comes alive!

Old stones chuckle, moss on their backs,
Sharing gossip of the woodland packs,
In stillness, there's a jelly-like dance,
As night hugs the grove, and dreams take a chance.

Reflections of Time in Twilight

Under purple skies, a party starts,
With frogs in tuxedos, colorful arts,
The past and present in a gentle swirl,
As time ticks on, giving laughter a twirl.

A brook babbles secrets, ticklish and sly,
Echoing giggles, they float on by,
Beneath the branches, a raccoon peeks,
With a glimmer of mischief, and comical squeaks.

Crickets dance, in shoes made of leaves,
Twisting and turning, in joyous reprieves,
While shadows play tag in fading light,
Creating patterns of pure delight.

The moon smiles down, a round, bright friend,
As night wraps the grove, this fun won't end,
With whimsy and laughter, such joyous glee,
In twilight's embrace, wild hearts run free.

The Gentle Rhythm of the Wilds

In the heart of green, where silliness flows,
The wildflowers chatter, gossiping grows,
Bees in bow ties buzz by with glee,
Sipping nectar, as sweet as can be.

A deer tiptoes, a playful prance,
She copies the bunny in a ballet dance,
While dandelions drift, like little gold ships,
Carried by giggles from bare little lips.

The brook giggles softly, tickling stones,
As fish in tuxedos practice their tones,
With splashes and flicks, they leap and dive,
Bringing joy to the woods, keeping laughter alive.

So here in the wilds, where spirit runs free,
Life dances along with such giddy spree,
In whispers, in rustles, the rhythm stays,
An echo of fun in the sunlight's rays.

www.ingramcontent.com/pod-product-compliance
Lightning Source LLC
Chambersburg PA
CBHW071849160426
43209CB00003B/482